DK SUPER World

BRAZIL

From the Amazon rainforest to the samba-filled streets of Rio de Janeiro, take an exciting adventure through Brazil

PRODUCED FOR DK BY

Editorial Caroline Wakeman Literary Agency
Design Collaborate Agency
Graphic story illustrator Matt Garbutt

Project Editor Amanda Eisenthal
Senior Art Editor Gilda Pacitti
Managing Editor Carine Tracanelli
Managing Art Editor Sarah Corcoran
Production Editor Robert Dunn
Production Controller Rebecca Parton
Publisher Sarah Forbes
Managing Director, Learning Hilary Fine

First American Edition, 2025
Published in the United States by DK Publishing,
a division of Penguin Random House LLC
1745 Broadway, 20th Floor, New York, NY 10019

Copyright © 2025 Dorling Kindersley Limited
25 26 27 28 29 10 9 8 7 6 5 4 3 2 1
001–345886–Jun/2025

All rights reserved.
Without limiting the rights under the copyright reserved above, no part of this publication may be reproduced, stored in or introduced into a retrieval system, or transmitted, in any form, or by any means (electronic, mechanical, photocopying, recording, or otherwise), without the prior written permission of the copyright owner.

Published in Great Britain by Dorling Kindersley Limited

A catalog record for this book is
available from the Library of Congress.
HC ISBN: 978-0-5939-6641-9
PB ISBN: 978-0-5939-6640-2

DK books are available at special discounts when purchased in bulk for sales promotions, premiums, fund-raising, or educational use.
For details, contact: DK Publishing Special Markets,
1745 Broadway, 20th Floor, New York, NY 10019
SpecialSales@dk.com

Printed and bound in China

www.dk.com

This book was made with Forest Stewardship Council™ certified paper – one small step in DK's commitment to a sustainable future.
Learn more at www.dk.com/uk/information/sustainability

CONTENTS

MAP — 4
Brazil

FACT FILE — 6
All About Brazil

TERRAINS — 8
Rainforests, Rivers, and Wetlands

LANDMARKS — 10
Iguaçu Falls

FLORA AND FAUNA — 12
Amazonian Animals and Super Predators

CULTURE — 18
Diversity, Entertainment, and Sports

RELIGION — 22
Catholicism, Candomblé, and Shamanism

NATIONAL HOLIDAYS AND FESTIVALS — 24
Light, Color, Carnival!

FOOD AND DRINK — 26
Stews, Seafood, and Sweet Treats

RECIPE — 28
Brigadeiros

HOME, WORK, AND SCHOOL — 30
Cities, Schools, and Industry

SCHOOL DAY DIARY — 32
Izabela's Day

HISTORY — 36
Colonization, Freedom, Democracy

HOW NIGHT CAME FROM THE OCEAN — 38

VOCABULARY BUILDER — 42
Fruits of Brazil

GLOSSARY — 44

INDEX — 46

Words in **bold** are explained in the glossary on page 44.

MAP

BRAZIL

Brazil is the largest country in South America. It is home to the world's biggest **rainforest**: the Amazon. Brazil has vibrant wildlife, landscapes, food, and celebrations. It is split into 26 states and one **federal district.**

FASCINATING FACT!

The Amazon rainforest is not just the biggest rainforest in the world, but the most **biodiverse**, too. It contains 10 percent of all wildlife species on Earth!

FACT FILE

ALL ABOUT BRAZIL

Bandeira do Brasil

- ⚑ Flag: Bandeira do Brasil
- 📍 Capital city: Brasília
- 👤 Population: Approx. 216 million
- 💬 Official language: Portuguese
- 💵 Currency: Real R$
- 🌳 National tree: Pau-brasil, also called Brazilwood
- ⬤ National dish: *Feijoada*
- 🐦 National bird: Rufous-bellied thrush
- 🎵 National anthem: "Hino Nacional Brasileiro" ("Brazilian National Anthem")
- ☆ Major exports: Soyabeans, corn, sugar, petroleum

FASCINATING FACT!

The rufous-bellied thrush helps the rainforests to grow. It eats ripe fruits and then spits out the seeds, planting new fruit trees.

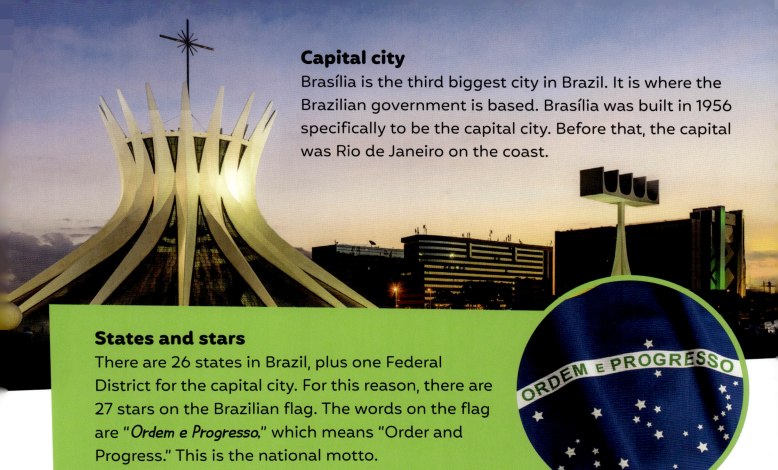

Capital city
Brasília is the third biggest city in Brazil. It is where the Brazilian government is based. Brasília was built in 1956 specifically to be the capital city. Before that, the capital was Rio de Janeiro on the coast.

States and stars
There are 26 states in Brazil, plus one Federal District for the capital city. For this reason, there are 27 stars on the Brazilian flag. The words on the flag are "*Ordem e Progresso,*" which means "Order and Progress." This is the national motto.

Language
Brazil is the only South American country that speaks Portuguese. Brazilian Portuguese is pronounced differently to European Portuguese, and some of the terms are different. For example, in Portugal, "train" is *comboio*, while in Brazil, it's *trem.*

Equator

FiND OuT!
Brazil is so big it shares a border with every other country in South America except two. Can you name these two countries?

Answer: Chile and Ecuador

Equatorial land
Brazil is mostly in the Southern **Hemisphere** just below the **equator**. In the Southern Hemisphere, the summers last from about December to March and the winters last from June to September.

TERRAINS

RAINFORESTS, RIVERS, AND WETLANDS

Brazil is the fifth-biggest country in the world. It has **tropical** climates in the north and **subtropical** climates further south. This allows for varied terrains, from vast rainforests to long coasts, and marshy wetlands to dry savannas.

Amazon rainforest
The Amazon rainforest has almost 400 billion trees. **Ecologically**, the Amazon is incredibly important, as it is home to millions of species of plants and animals. It also absorbs more than 40 percent of all the **carbon dioxide** in the world.

Amazon River
The Amazon River is the second longest river on Earth. During the wet season, the river can be up to 31 miles (50 km) wide! The river runs right through the Amazon rainforest from east to west. It is joined by around 1,100 **tributaries** before it drains into the Atlantic Ocean.

Wetlands
The Pantanal is a vast tropical **wetland** of about 81,000 square miles (210,000 sq km)—that's about the size of Kansas, USA. Each year, the Pantanal fills up during rainy season and slowly drains away during the dry season. It's a refuge for around 10 million **caimans**.

Savanna
The Cerrado in central Brazil is the most biodiverse savanna in the world. A savanna is a shrubby plain of grassland with scattered trees. It gets dry winters and rainy summers, which makes it an excellent place for varied plant life. However, nearly half of the Cerrado vegetation is lost due to over-farming.

FASCINATING FACT!

A new animal or plant species is found in the Amazon rainforest an average of once every other day.

Coasts
Brazil's 4,654-mile (7,491-km) coastline along the Atlantic Ocean has some of the most famous, and longest, golden sandy beaches in the world. On the coast in the north, you'll find the unique Lençóis Maranhense National Park, with rolling white sand dunes and lagoons of emerald-green water.

LANDMARKS

IGUAÇU FALLS

The Iguaçu Falls is the largest waterfall system in the entire world. It is made up of around 275 individual waterfalls that range in size up to 269 feet (82 m) tall. The Falls form part of the border between Brazil and its southern neighbor Argentina.

The Devil's Throat
Of the hundreds of individual waterfalls, perhaps the most famous is the Garganta del Diablo ("Devil's Throat"). It is a huge horseshoe-shaped fall right in the heart of the Iguaçu Falls system. The shape of the Devil's Throat helps sound to echo and vibrate, generating an almighty roar and giving the waterfall its name.

Formation of the Falls

Millions of years ago, volcanoes erupted over a desert to form the Paraná Plateau: a surface of extremely hard **basaltic** rock over layers of very soft **sandstone**. Movements in the earth formed cracks, and the Iguaçu River flowed through those cracks. This **eroded** the softer rock while the hard basaltic rock formed steep cliffs.

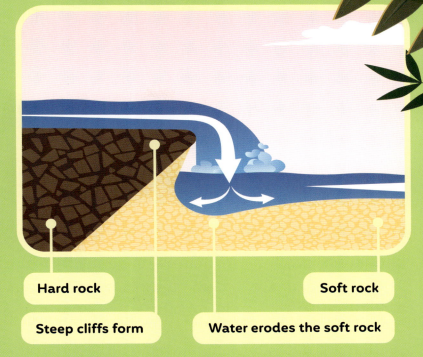

Hard rock

Soft rock

Steep cliffs form

Water erodes the soft rock

FASCINATING FACT!

The splashing water of the Falls creates a mist of rainbows 500 feet (150 m) high.

Parks and wildlife

Besides the waterfalls, Iguaçu National Park has hundreds of miles of rainforests and other wild land. The park has an abundance of wildlife, including animals that are rarely seen elsewhere, like giant anteaters and jaguarundis. It also has more than 600 species of butterfly!

FLORA AND FAUNA

AMAZONIAN ANIMALS AND SUPER PREDATORS

Brazil has some of the most diverse wildlife of any natural space. New species are being found all the time. Unfortunately, due to **deforestation** and the farming **industry**, wild habitats are under threat.

IN THE TREETOPS

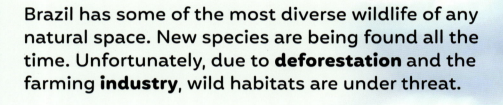

Hyacinth macaw

Toco toucan
At 2 feet (60 cm) long, these big birds are the largest toucan species. Their curved orange beaks are almost a third of their body length. When they sleep, they tuck their beaks under their wings to keep warm. Toucans are not great flyers, so they mostly hop about in the treetops.

Harpy eagle

These raptors are so strong they can snatch sloths and monkeys from the rainforest canopy and carry them off. Their eyesight is eight times better than a human's, and they are so agile they can fly through the treetops at 50 miles per hour (80 kph).

Golden lion tamarin

These tiny monkeys are **endemic** to the Atlantic forests of Brazil. They are about the size of a squirrel and have bright golden fur and a tufted mane. Golden lion tamarins live in small family groups. They forage mainly on fruits, insects, and small mammals.

Maned sloth

These sloths have three toes and a long black mane. Maned sloths are very slow creatures that travel an average of just 125 feet (38 m) a day. They are rare, found only in the coastal forests of Brazil. Their habitat is under constant threat from deforestation. To safely hang upside down for long periods of time, special blood vessels help pump oxygen, and their organs are attached to their ribs so they don't get squashed.

WATERY WILDLIFE

Yacaré caiman

Caiman
Yacaré and spectacled caimans are found in huge numbers in the Pantanal wetlands. They are the favorite prey of ferocious jaguars. The yacaré males are about 8 feet (2.5 m) and spectacled males about 6.5 feet (2 m). The females are slightly smaller.

Pink river dolphin
Also known as *boto*, these dolphins are found only in the Amazon. The bulb on their heads helps them use **echolocation** to hunt fish in the muddy Amazon waters. Their thin, sharp teeth can crack open turtle shells.

Red-bellied piranha
These Amazonian fish have sharp, interlocking teeth that give them a powerful bite. They are mainly scavengers and eat small fish, insects, plants, and seeds. In rare cases, they can swarm in groups to take down larger animals that are sick or injured.

Giant Amazon waterlily
Victoria amazonica have platform-like leaves that float on the water. They can reach 10 feet (3 m) across and can support the weight of a golden retriever. The undersides of the pads trap air to help them float.

Anaconda
These snakes live both in the water and on the land. The heaviest anaconda ever recorded weighed 500 pounds (227 kg)! That's as much as a full-grown tiger. They are constrictors, which means they hunt by wrapping their bodies around their prey to suffocate them.

Capybara
These are the biggest rodents in the world, measuring up to 4.6 feet (1.4 m) long! They wallow in the Pantanal and have webbed toes for swimming. Their eyes are high on their heads so they can check above the water for danger.

Capybara
4.6 feet (1.4 m)

Human
5.6 feet (1.7 m)

Jaguar
6 feet (1.8 m)

Yacaré caiman
8 feet (2.5 m)

Spectacled caiman
6.5 feet (2 m)

Waterlily
10 feet (3 m)

Anaconda
20 feet (6 m)

RAINFOREST WILDERNESS

Giant anteater
At more than 6.5 feet (2 m) long, giant anteaters have to eat tens of thousands of ants a day to survive! They have no teeth but use their huge claws to dig at ant and termite nests. A 2-foot (60 cm) long tongue snatches out ants.

Brazil nut tree
These trees have a **mutualistic relationship** with rodents called agouties who have sharp teeth that break into the tough shell of the nuts. Agouties then store the nuts for future. The ones they forget about become new trees.

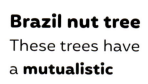

Jaguar
These large cats are deadly hunters. They are strong swimmers and live in tropical forests near water. They hunt ground animals like armadillos, deer, and monkeys, as well as water prey like caimans and turtles. Their powerful jaws can bite through bone and shells.

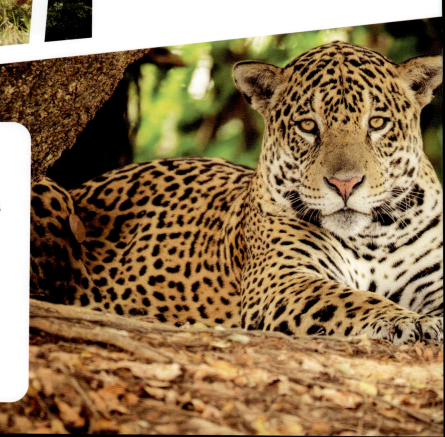

ENDANGERED SPECIES

Deforestation

Palicourea elata is better known as "hot lips" because the bright red leaves grow in the shape of a pair of lips. Deforestation for the farming industry has caused the plant to become **endangered**. It is medicinal and can treat rashes, earaches, and coughs.

Pollution

Giant otters are sleek, playful mammals native to the Amazon River and Pantanal wetlands. They are hunters who play a key role in the **ecosystem**, but they are also reducing in number. Much of this is due to pollution in the water from mining and agriculture.

Habitat loss

Maned wolves have long legs and a black mane that stands on end when they feel threatened. Maned wolf **populations** are in decline because so much of their grassland and rainforest habitats are cleared and used for farmland.

17

CULTURE

DIVERSITY, ENTERTAINMENT, AND SPORTS

Brazilian culture is a rich mix. Its deep history involves Indigenous peoples, Portuguese **colonization**, a long trade in **enslaved** people from Africa, and immigration from around the world. Today, almost half the population identify as mixed-race. All of this has led to a huge variety of music, dance, food, and customs.

FASCINATING FACT!

Brazil has the largest Japanese population outside of Japan itself.

DIVERSITY

Indigenous tribe village in the state of Amazonas

Indigenous
There are around 1.7 million Indigenous people living in Brazil. Indigenous communities have a huge variety of languages, customs, beliefs, and lifestyles. The largest group is the Guaraní. Almost all of their land has been lost and stolen since European colonization.

African
African influences are everywhere! African spices and techniques are used for cooking classic Brazilian dishes. Afro-Brazilian dances and music styles like samba are very popular. The colors, costumes, and customs in celebrations like Carnival have deep African influences.

Portuguese-style architecture in the Pelourinho district of Salvador, Bahia

European
About 45 percent of the population identify as white with European **heritage.** European roots are mostly Portuguese, but there are also strong German and Italian connections. The European influence can be seen in the Portuguese language, architecture, customs, and love of soccer.

19

ENTERTAINMENT

Telenovelas
This is a kind of TV show that's enormously popular in Brazil. The shows are set in the real world and often have dramatic, emotional plots and a familiar cast of characters. There is a focus on romance and family, and on revealed secrets!

Samba
Samba is both a type of dance and a type of music. It originated with enslaved African communities. Dancers wear vivid colors and feathered headdresses. The dance involves rapid foot and hip movements led by African drumming rhythms. Samba is especially important at the Carnival festival.

Beach life!
Brazil has some of the most famous beaches in the world, like Copacabana and Ipanema. People will arrive early and spend their whole day at the beach. They might chat with friends, surf, play volleyball, and eat and drink at the many beach kiosks.

SPORTS

Capoeira
This is a martial art in which fighting movements are performed to music and drumming. It was invented by enslaved Africans to disguise the fact that they were practicing self-defense. After slavery was **abolished** in 1888, the government found capoeira so threatening they made it illegal for 40 years!

Futebol!
Soccer, or *futebol* in Portuguese, is the nation's favorite sport. Brazil has won the FIFA World Cup more times than any other country. Soccer was introduced by Scottish immigrants in the late 1800s. Since then, Brazil has been soccer mad.

Mixed martial arts
This sport, known as MMA, combines techniques from various fighting styles. In Brazil, the main techniques come from Brazilian jiu-jitsu, where the focus is on grappling. MMA fighters are also skilled in kickboxing, karate, wrestling, and more.

RELIGION

CATHOLICISM, CANDOMBLÉ, AND SHAMANISM

Catholicism is the main religion of Brazil, brought over by the Portuguese. The religions Candomblé and Umbanda are uniquely Afro-Brazilian and stem from enslaved communities. The hundreds of Indigenous communities all have their own beliefs and practices.

Catholicism
Catholicism is a type of Christianity. Christians worship Jesus Christ, the son of an almighty god. Catholics also follow the Pope, a spiritual leader based in Rome. Catholics believe that confessing your sins will allow God to forgive you. Catholic religious rituals are called sacraments.

Catedral da Sé

Candomblé

Candomblé is an Afro-Brazilian religion that stemmed from African beliefs. Followers worship *orixás*: spirits of nature and human life, such as thunder, family, and love. Oludumaré is the supreme creator, and Yemanjá is the goddess of the sea. Candomblé ceremonies are full of music and dancing.

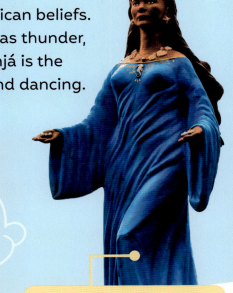

A statue of Yemanjá

 FASCINATING FACT!

Enslaved people had to hide their Candomblé faith, which was made illegal until the 1970s. They had to pretend to be Catholics and incorporate Catholic icons in their worship.

Umbanda

This Afro-Brazilian religion blends African beliefs with Catholic and Indigenous elements. Umbanda has *orixás* alongside Indigenous spirits, Catholic saints, spirits of past enslaved people, and a god called Olorun.

Shamanism and spiritualism

Religions and beliefs in Indigenous tribes are diverse and varied. Some might worship spirits that inhabit animals and elements of nature. Many tribes also have shamans: holy people who act as advisors, healers, and scholars. Shamans sometimes communicate between the human and spiritual worlds.

Rituals and ceremonies

Indigenous peoples have many practices. In the Ticuna tribe, when girls reach a certain age, they dance over fires for days before learning their people's history. Shamans of the Awá tribe use clapping and chanting to go into a trance and commune with the spirits.

NATIONAL HOLIDAYS AND FESTIVALS

LIGHT, COLOR, CARNIVAL!

Brazil is a country that loves to celebrate! Their holidays and festivals are often vibrant and colorful, full of music and dancing.

Carnival (Carnaval do Brasil)
Held in spring, Carnival is the biggest festival in Brazil. It is celebrated with five days of parties, music, dancing, sparkly costumes, and food and drink. There are huge parades of samba dancers in feathery costumes, and even the spectators dress up!

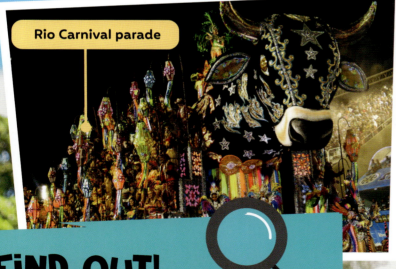

Rio Carnival parade

FIND OUT!

The biggest Carnival celebration is in Rio de Janeiro, where millions of people take part. Can you find out what state Rio de Janeiro is in?

Answer: Rio de Janeiro state!

Black Consciousness Day
(Dia da Consciência Negra)
November 20 honors Brazil's Afro-Brazilian population. It is a day to celebrate the culture, history, and community of Afro-Brazilians, and to recognize the struggles of Black communities. The date honors Zumbi dos Palmares, a formerly enslaved person who fought to abolish slavery.

Independence Day
(Dia da Independência)
On September 7, Brazilians celebrate the anniversary of Brazil's independence from Portugal, beginning in 1822. People take part in parades and enjoy fireworks.

Corpus Christi
60 days after Easter, Brazilians celebrate the Christian holiday of Corpus Christi. People make carpets called *tapetes de rua* to decorate the streets. Different cities use different materials, including flowers, colored sawdust, embroidery, sand, and even coffee.

Bonfim Stairs Washing
(Lavagem do Bonfim)
In Salvador, on the second Thursday of January, people dressed in white walk 5 miles (8 km) to the Church of Nosso Senhor do Bonfim. Baianas (Afro-Brazilian women from Bahia) carry jars of water and wash the steps of the church. The celebration has elements of both Catholic and Afro-Brazilian cultures.

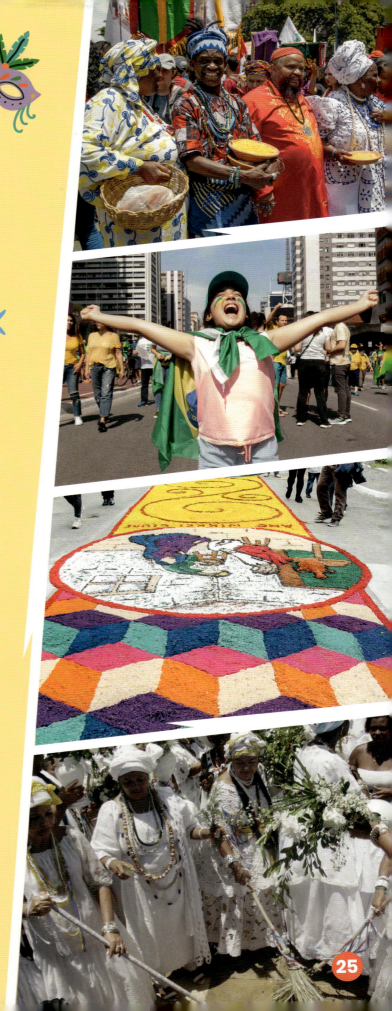

 **FOOD AND DRINK**

STEWS, SEAFOOD, AND SWEET TREATS

Brazilian cuisine is a blend of influences from Indigenous, African, and European peoples. There is a wide variety of flavors, aromas, and textures. Dishes from particular regions reflect local traditions.

Cassava
Also known as yuca, tapioca, and manioc, this is a root vegetable used in a lot of Brazilian cooking. Some popular forms are cassava fries, mashed cassava, and *farofa*—a side dish made from toasted cassava flour.

Farofa

Feijoada
This is a stew of black beans and meats cooked slowly over a few hours. It is considered Brazil's national dish. The name comes from the Portuguese *feijão* meaning beans.

Pão de queijo
The name translates to "cheese bread." These are small balls of soft white bread filled with cheese. Cassava flour is used, which gives the balls a bit of a chew and a crunch!

Brigadeiro
This is a classic Brazilian treat! It is made with chocolate powder, butter, and condensed milk, rolled into a ball and coated in chocolate sprinkles.

Guaraná soda
This is an energy drink made from the seeds of the guaraná plant. The Sateré-Mawé people of the Amazon were the first to farm it and make a drink called *çapó*.

Moqueca
This is a fish stew. Different regions have different versions. *Moqueca* from Bahia, for example, is African-influenced and uses palm oil, coconut milk, and local fish.

Chimarrão
This hot drink is made from the leaves of the yerba mate tree. It is bright green, herby, and creamy. The drink originated with Indigenous cultures, in particular the Guaraní and Tupi peoples.

Acarajé
This street food is a bean fritter that's fried and stuffed with spicy pastes or fillings like shrimp or vegetables. It has African origins and is often sold by Baianas: Afro-Brazilian women from Bahia.

RECIPE

BRIGADEIROS

These little chocolate balls are a popular treat in Brazil. They are often served at celebrations, like birthdays and weddings, or just as a simple treat! Some impatient people eat the chocolate mixture right out of the pot—this is known as *brigadeiro de colher* (spoon *brigadeiro*). This recipe makes about 30 *brigadeiros* to share.

Ingredients
- 14 oz (397 g) can of condensed milk
- 1 tbsp. (14 g) of butter
- 3 tbsp. (45 g) of cocoa powder (unsweetened)
- 1/3 cup (65 g) of sprinkles

Toppings
Try a few different toppings:
- Chocolate curls
- Chopped dried fruit
- Chopped nuts

Method

1. First, measure out your ingredients. Add the condensed milk, butter, and cocoa powder to a medium-sized saucepan.
2. Turn the heat to medium. Stir the mixture slowly as it starts to melt.
3. Keep stirring constantly for 10 to 15 minutes until the mixture starts to thicken. Don't let it burn!
4. The mixture is thick enough when you can run your spoon through it to see the bottom of the pan and it takes about 3 seconds for the mixture to flow back into place.
5. Leave the mixture to fully cool.
6. Make the balls! When it's cool, use your hands to form the mixture into golf ball-sized balls. If it's too sticky, you can use a little bit of oil on your hands to make it easier.
7. On a clean, dry surface like a baking sheet, spread out a sheet of sprinkles. Roll each ball in the sprinkles.
8. Enjoy immediately or put in the fridge to keep cool.

! **Be careful not to eat too much sugar in a day.**

A brief history

The story goes that *brigadeiros* were named for Brigadier Eduardo Gomes (a brigadier is an army officer), who ran for **president** in the 1940s. People wanted to sell treats to raise money for his **election**, but ingredients like chocolate and fresh milk were hard to find after World War II. This recipe was invented using ingredients they could find easily.

HOME, WORK, AND SCHOOL

CITIES, SCHOOLS, AND INDUSTRY

São Paulo

Brazil is a huge country with diverse ways of living. About 88 percent of the population live in cities, and Brazil has some of the biggest cities in the world. While some Indigenous people live in forests, savannas, and other natural spaces, some also live in urban areas.

Favelas
Many cities have areas of crowded housing called *favelas.* These developed as people moved to the cities in search of work. There was not enough access to housing, so people had to build their own. *Favelas* continue to grow today, and many lack consistent water and electricity supplies. *Favela* communities often have a strong art and cultural scene.

Farming

More than a third of all coffee in the world is produced in Brazil in one of the 300,000 **plantations**. Brazil also grows enormous amounts of soyabeans, 75 percent of which goes to feed animals on farms. Cattle farming is another major industry. Unfortunately, soyabean and cattle farming result in huge amounts of deforestation.

Schools

School in Brazil is free until the age of 17. In many public schools (*escolas públicas*), the day is short and has two shifts: a morning shift runs from about 7:30am to about 12:30pm, and then afternoon students attend from about 1pm to 6pm. Some of the busiest schools even have class in the evening.

School stages

Infant: 4–6 years old   **Elementary I:** 6–10 years old   **Elementary II:** 10–14 years old   **High:** 15–17 years old

Tourism

Tourism is a booming sector in Brazil. An estimated 6.5 million people visit each year to sample the food, culture, and climate. This feeds into businesses and the **economy**, but it can also have negative impacts on the environment and local communities.

SCHOOL DAY DIARY

IZABELA'S DAY

Name: Izabela Medeiros
Age: 11
Lives: São Paulo
Family: Mom, brother (Paulo), sister (Sophia)

Olá! My name is Izabela, and this is my day in 5th grade.

School starts at 7:30am so I get up at 6 and get ready. The sun is already up. I have cereal for breakfast and help my little brother Paulo get ready. My mom drives us to school before she goes to work. I help Paulo and Sophia with their things before I go to my classroom.

Sophia (Younger sister)   Paulo (Younger brother)
Me   Mom

I always sit with Carla and Bruno. When the bell rings at 7:30, the Portuguese teacher arrives. Today we write a pretend letter to make an argument about something. I am arguing that there are too many *telenovelas* in the evening. They are boring and should be aired later, when children have gone to bed.

Telenovela: A dramatic TV show for adults.

Next, we have math. We have a different teacher for each subject, and they come to our classroom when it is time for the class so we don't have to move.

After that, it's recess (*recreio*)! We go outside and have our snacks. I have a cheese sandwich and a banana and eat it quick so we can play soccer (*futebol*). We play King of the Street (*Rei da Rua*): the king is in goal and we take turns taking shots. If the king saves it, they stay in goal. If a kid scores, they are in goal. Whoever is king the longest wins!

At 10 o'clock, the bells goes and we go back in for geography. We are making posters about deforestation. That's when trees are chopped down to make space for things like cattle farming. This is really bad because animals lose their homes and because the forests provide us with oxygen.

In the afternoon, we have history. History is my favorite because so much has happened! The last class is art. We have to clear away really well because in the afternoon a different set of students arrives to start their school day.

My mom comes to pick us up, and Bruno too because he's coming to my house. We have *arroz e feijão* with stewed chicken for lunch and then go to the park to meet my neighbors. Sophia comes too but Paulo always has a nap when it's hot after school. We put out goals but we only have six people so we play without anyone in goal. I'm practicing dribbling with my left foot.

Arroz e feijão: Rice and beans. This is a common side dish.

When the sun starts to get really low, I know it's nearly time for Bruno's dad to get him, so we go back home. In October, the sun sets at around 6pm. When Bruno is gone, I do my homework and finish my letter for Portuguese class.

Farofa: A side dish of toasted cassava flour.

We all sit down at the table for dinner. We are having fish stew (*moqueca*) with rice and *farofa*.
We usually spend quite a long time eating and talking. Then Sophia and I play one of her educational video games while Paulo and Mom watch TV. I get ready for bed and read a bit and then it's lights out!

Good night (*boa noite*).

Fish stew (*moqueca*)

HISTORY

COLONIZATION, FREEDOM, DEMOCRACY

People have existed in Brazil for at least 35,000 years. Before Europeans, Indigenous peoples like the Tupi and Guaraní were the biggest communities. It is estimated that between 2 and 11 million people were living in Brazil before contact with the Portuguese.

Pedro Álvares Cabral

Portuguese contact
The Portuguese arrived in 1500 CE, led by Pedro Álvares Cabral. Many Indigenous people were killed by warfare and diseases brought from Europe. The Portuguese established a **colony** and made attempts to enslave Indigenous people. They mined gold and diamonds and sent sugar and red dye back to Europe to sell.

FASCINATING FACT!

One of the oldest human skeletons found was discovered in a cave in Brazil. She was called Luzia and dated back 11,000 years.

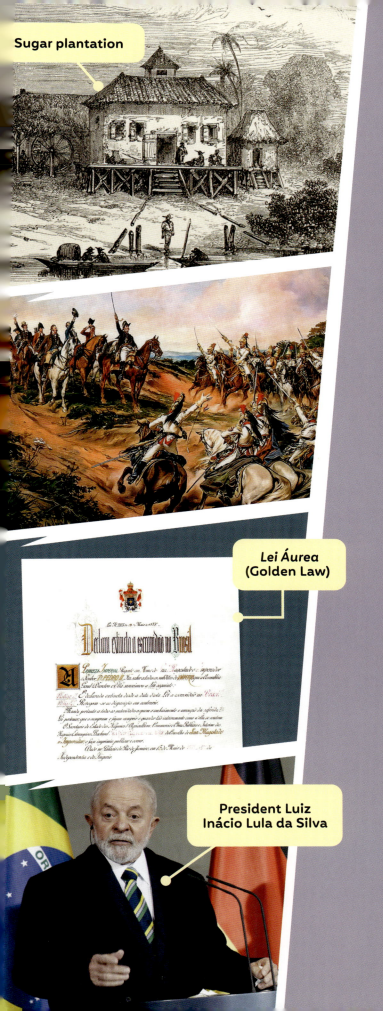

Sugar plantation

Lei Áurea (Golden Law)

President Luiz Inácio Lula da Silva

Start of slavery
The Portuguese enslaved people from Africa to work on plantations. Brazil imported more than 5 million enslaved people over 300 years. Enslaved people survived and resisted by preserving their own languages, dances, music, and food.

War of Independence
Prince Pedro I of Portugal was left to rule Brazil in 1820. In 1822, after the Brazilian people protested against Portuguese rule, Prince Pedro announced Brazil's independence. After three years of fighting, Portugal acknowledged Brazilian independence in 1825.

End of slavery and monarchy
The Golden Law abolished slavery in 1888, after decades of fighting by activists and *quilombos* (communities of escaped enslaved people). In 1889, the **monarchy** was overthrown by military leaders. This began the era of presidents.

Rise of democracy
Brazil suffered a series of corrupt leaders and **dictators** in the 1900s. Elections were often not fair or did not happen at all. In 1988, a new **constitution** gave people the right to vote in fair elections. Today, Brazil is a growing economy led by an elected president.

HOW NIGHT CAME FROM THE OCEAN

In the beginning there was no night. Only day.

The princess of the ocean left her underwater home to marry a prince of the land.

At first, they were happy. But the longer she stayed in the bright sun, the weaker she became.

I need the darkness of the deep ocean, but I am too weak to return my father, the Great Sea Serpent.

I will send my brothers! Please, go to the Great Sea Serpent and ask for darkness for his daughter.

Yes!

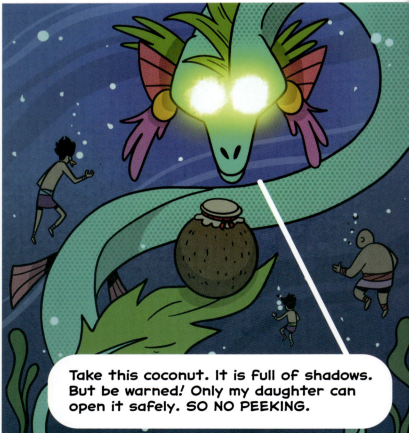

Take this coconut. It is full of shadows. But be warned! Only my daughter can open it safely. SO NO PEEKING.

In the darkness, the princess felt better at once.

"Ahhh..."

But the darkness did not lift. The people grew frightened. Plants began to wilt and animals called out in distress.

HOOT HOOT GRRROWL

The princess knew she had to separate the night from the day, so she made a bird for the day.

"You will sing for the dawn."

"You will sing for the dusk."

And a bird for the night.

"You three! You disobeyed the Great Sea Serpent and almost doomed us all!"

POP POP

The princess turned them into animals!

And so the cycle of night and day began.

VOCABULARY BUILDER

FRUITS OF BRAZIL

From its many forests and jungles, Brazil has more than 300 different kinds of colorful, native fruits to offer. Read these tantalizing descriptions of some of the fruits.

Maracujá
This is a plump oval fruit that can be pale orange, soft yellow, deep purple, or green. Inside, the wet seeds have a sweet tropical flavor.

Caju
This bell-shaped fruit is stringy, juicy, and has a sweet taste that's also a bit tangy. The olive-green cashew nut grows out of the top.

Jabuticaba
This firm, blackish-purple fruit looks similar to a grape, but has tougher, darker skin. Inside, the flesh is pearly white. It has a floral taste that's a bit peppery.

Guaraná
This has a hard, bumped shell that's a vibrant red. The fruit looks like an eye! It tastes slightly bitter.

Carambola
This is a long, ridged, star-shaped fruit. Its skin is waxy. It is sweet, citrussy, and a bit sour.

42

What do the fruits taste like?
bitter, citrussy, floral, juicy, peppery, sour, sweet, tangy, tropical

How are the colors described?
black, deep, green, orange, pale, pearly, purple, red, vibrant, white, yellow

What textures are described?
bumped, firm, hard, plump, ridged, soft, stringy, tough, waxy, wet

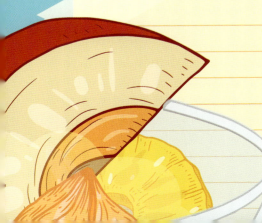

Design your own fruit salad! Choose from the fruits above or add some of your favorites, such as strawberries or apples. Write a description of your fruit salad using the vocabulary boxes to help you.
- How do the different fruits look?
- How do they taste?

43

GLOSSARY

Abolished Officially ended.

Basalt Hard, black, volcanic rock.

Biodiversity Variety in plant and animal life.

Caiman A reptile related to the crocodile, but smaller than a crocodile.

Carbon dioxide A gas given off by using fossil fuels.

Colonization The act of taking control of a land and settling by force, often displacing people who already exist there.

Colony A settlement created by people from another country or area.

Constitution A document that sets out the laws, beliefs, and rules for a country.

Deforestation The clearing of forested areas.

Democracy A form of government in which the people in power are elected by the general population.

Dictator A ruler with total power over a country.

Echolocation The ability to locate items and environments using sound.

Ecological Relating to the environment and ecosystems.

Economy A system of making money and producing goods and services.

Ecosystem A community of plants, animals, and other environmental factors that exist together and have relationships and interactions that affect each other.

Election A public vote.

Endangered At risk of extinction.

Endemic Native to a specific area or country and mainly or only found in that area or country.

Enslave To force someone to work for little or no pay and exclude them from human rights.

Equator An imaginary line around the Earth that is exactly halfway between the North and South Poles.

Erosion When wind, water, ice, or other natural pressures wear away at rock.

Federal district A region of a country that is used as the base for the central government.

Hemisphere Regions north or south of the equator. There is the Northern Hemisphere and the Southern Hemisphere.

Heritage History, traditions, beliefs, and practices that are inherited from the past.

Industry A particular area or type of business. For example, the automobile industry refers to the manufacture and sale of vehicles.

Monarchy A system of royalty with a head, such as a king or queen.

Mutualistic relationship When two organisms from different species work together beneficially for survival.

Plantation A farm or estate that grows a particular crop, such as coffee or bananas.

President An elected leader of a country. It can also mean the leader of an organization or company.

Rainforest A tropical forest that gets a lot of rain.

Sandstone A rock formed from sand.

Subtropical Related to regions close to the tropics (the area around the equator), usually with mild-to-hot weather that changes with the seasons.

Tourism When people travel away from their home to see other places. The tourism industry involves travel, hotels, restaurants, and attractions.

Tributaries Smaller water systems, like streams or small rivers, that flow into a larger water system, like a large river or lake.

Tropical Related to regions around the equator, usually with hot and humid weather all year.

Wetland Flooded area of land that is marshy and swampy.

INDEX

A
acarajé 27
African influences 19, 20, 21, 23, 27
Afro-Brazilians 19, 22, 23, 25, 27
agouties 16
Amazon rainforest 4, 5, 8, 9
Amazon River 5, 8, 14, 17
anacondas 15
Argentina 10
Atlantic Ocean 8, 9

B
Bahia 19, 25, 27
Baianas 25, 27
basalt 11
beaches 9, 20
biodiversity 5, 9
Black Consciousness Day 25
Bonfim 25
Brasília 4, 5, 6, 7
Brazil nut tree 16
brigadeiros 27, 28–29
butterflies 11

C
Cabral, Pedro Álvares 36
caimans 9, 14, 15, 16
Candomblé 22, 23
capoeira 21
capybaras 15
carbon dioxide 8
Carnival (Carnaval) 19, 20, 24

cassava 26, 27, 35
Catholicism 22, 23, 25
celebrations 24–25, 28
Cerrado 9
chimarrão 27
cities 7, 25, 30
climate 8
coastline 9, 13
coffee production 31
colonization 18, 19, 36
Corpus Christi 25
culture 18–21

D
deforestation 12, 13, 17, 31, 33
 see also over-farming
democracy 37
Devil's Throat 10
dictators 37
dolphins 14
drinks 27

E
echolocation 14
ecosystem 17
education 31
endangered species 17
entertainment 20
European influences 19, 26
exports 6, 31

F
farming 9, 17, 31, 33
farofa 26, 35
fauna 6, 9, 11, 12–17

favelas 30
federal district 4, 7
feijoada 6, 26
flag 6, 7
flora 9, 15, 16
food 26–29, 42–43
forests 13, 11, 16, 17, 30
 see also deforestation
fruits 42–43
futebol 21, 33

G
giant anteaters 11, 16
giant otters 17
golden lion tamarins 13
Gomes, Eduardo 29
governance 37
guaraná sodas 27
Guaraní 19, 27, 36

H
habitat loss 17
harpy eagles 13
history 36–37
hot lips (*Palicourea elata*) 17

I
Iguaçu Falls 5, 10–11
Iguaçu National Park 11
Iguaçu River 10, 11
independence 37
Independence Day 25
Indigenous peoples 18, 19, 22, 23, 26, 27, 30, 36
industries 31

J
jaguars 14, 16
jaguarundis 11
Japanese population 18

L
Lençóis Maranhenses National Park 9
Luzia 36

M
maned sloths 13
maned wolves 17
mixed martial arts (MMA) 21
monarchy 37
moqueca 27, 35

N
national dish 6, 26
national parks 9, 11

O
over-farming 9

P
pães de queijo, 27
Pantanal 9, 14, 15, 17
Paraná Plateau 11
Pedro I 37
pink river dolphin 14
piranhas 14
plantations 31, 37
pollution 17
population distribution 30

Portugal 25
Portuguese language 7, 19, 21
Portuguese people 22, 36–37
presidents 37

Q
quilombos 37

R
rainforests 11, 13, 16, 17
 see also Amazon rainforest
red-bellied piranhas 14
religion 22–23
Rio de Janeiro 4, 7, 24
rufous-bellied thrush 6

S
samba 19, 20, 24
sandstone 11
Sateré-Mawé 27
savannas 8, 9, 30
schools 31
Shamanism 23
slavery 23, 25, 36, 37
soccer 19, 21, 33
spiritualism 23
sports 21
Stairs Washing 25
states 4, 7

T
telenovelas 20, 32
terrains 8–9
toco toucans 12
tourism 31

trees 6, 8, 9, 16, 27
tributaries 8
Tupi 27, 36

U
Umbanda 22, 23

W
War of Independence 37
waterfalls 10–11
waterlilies, giant Amazon 15
wetlands 9, 14, 15, 17
work 31

Z
Zumbi dos Palmares 25

ACKNOWLEDGMENTS

The publisher would like to thank the following for their kind permission to reproduce their photographs:

(Key: a-above; b-below/bottom; c-centre; f-far; l-left; r-right; t-top)

Adobe Stock: Adilson 27clb, Aide 12br, Curioso.Photography 8crb, Drazen 21bl, Marcos 11cl, rjuniormb 27cra, Tarcisio Schnaider 16tr, StockImageBrasil 24, WS Studio 28-29, YoonazPhoto 11bl; **Alamy Stock Photo:** Niday Picture Library 37cla, Robertharding / Michael Nolan 17cr, Svintage Archive 37clb; **Depositphotos Inc:** marzolino 36; **Dreamstime.com:** 3djuuuice 32cr, Ernest Akayeu 20tr, 25c (x3), 42-43bc, Thales Antonio 21tl, Anna Artamonova 14bl, 19tl, Avictorero 15bc, Ayn1987 28bl, Tatiana Belova 14br, Buch 18-19 (Feather), Winkler Chaves 27cla, 42crb, Bonandbon Dw 19cr, Rudolf Ernst 19bl, Peter Hermes Furian 4cb, Diego Grandi 22, Ivanildo Huebl 10, Lazyllama 18, Leannevorrias 24clb, Lindrik 30br, Angela Macario 6, Macrovector 33b, Chernishev Maksim 20cl, Oduvaldo Mazza Junior 27cla (Soda), Anna Orlova 35b, Yuliya Pauliukevich 10-11 (Leaves), Potysiev 26cra, Ppy2010ha 27cr, Ondrej Prosicky 14t, Rodrigolab 20b, Giovanni Seabra 27br, Joa Souza 25br, Sriharun 42cr, Ssstocker 34c, Chalermchai Thaisamrong 43tr, Matthew Trommer 7cra, VectorMine 11tr, Wirestock 12; **Shutterstock.com:** 32 pixels 4bc, A.RICARDO 21cl, Alfmaler 5bc, Aratehortua 31cb, barbaliss 6t, Best Food Photos 27tl, Bibadash 22tr, Bigzumi 15cb, Fernando Calmon 9cr, Chepesch 17br, Chipmunk131 15bl (Human), creative photographer 11 13t, D1 Photography 29cra, Firsova Elena 29b, fabianomr 16b, Floratta 6bl, Gabriel Gabino 9tl, guentermanaus 17tc, Hasyimstok 31tr (cla), imageBROKER.com 7bl, Huang Jenhung 13bl, F de Jesus 23tr, 23cr, Latterry 15tl, lazyllama 31bl, Flavio Leao 25cra, Thiago Leite 30, Lucas Leuzinger 16tl, Golovina Marina 32-35 (Paper BG), Wilson Santos Marques 9b, Marzolino 37tl, Eduardo Menezes 13br, Marcelo Morena 16cra, Robert Napiorkowski 7t, Nataly Studio 42bc, Juergen Nowak 37bl, PARALAXIS 17tr, Martin Pelanek 15tr, PitukTV 20tr (TV), Erica Catarina Pontes 25crb, pukao 42c, rodrigobark 26ca, Albert Roman 26, Sashatigar 20 (Doodle), SelenaMay 15bl, TairA 43cl, Marco Tulio 42cb, VectorPunks 31cr, Wagner Vilas 25tr, Christian Vinces 8, Achim Wagner 36cra, Agung_Wibisono 32tr, 34bl, xenia_ok 32-34 (Pencil), Alena Zharava 31tl

Cover images: Front: **Getty Images / iStock:** Nirut Punshiri t; **Shutterstock.com:** Art Studio VN bl, Reforestation Collection br, Alf Ribeiro cr; Back: **Dreamstime.com:** Ivanildo Huebl tl, Lindrik bl; **Shutterstock.com:** fabianomr cl

All of the books in the *Super World* series have been reviewed by authenticity readers of the cultures represented to make sure they are culturally accurate.